NATIONAL GEOGRAPHIC

Little Monkeys

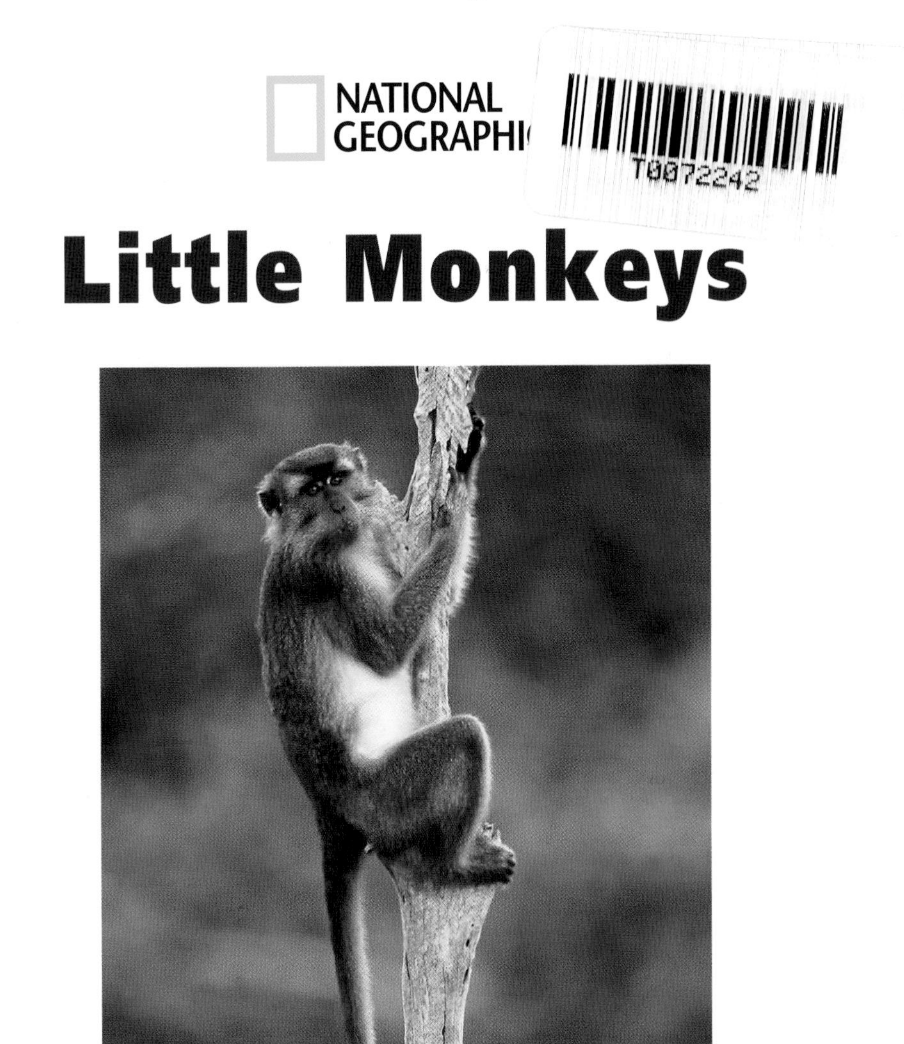

Gustav Blümchen

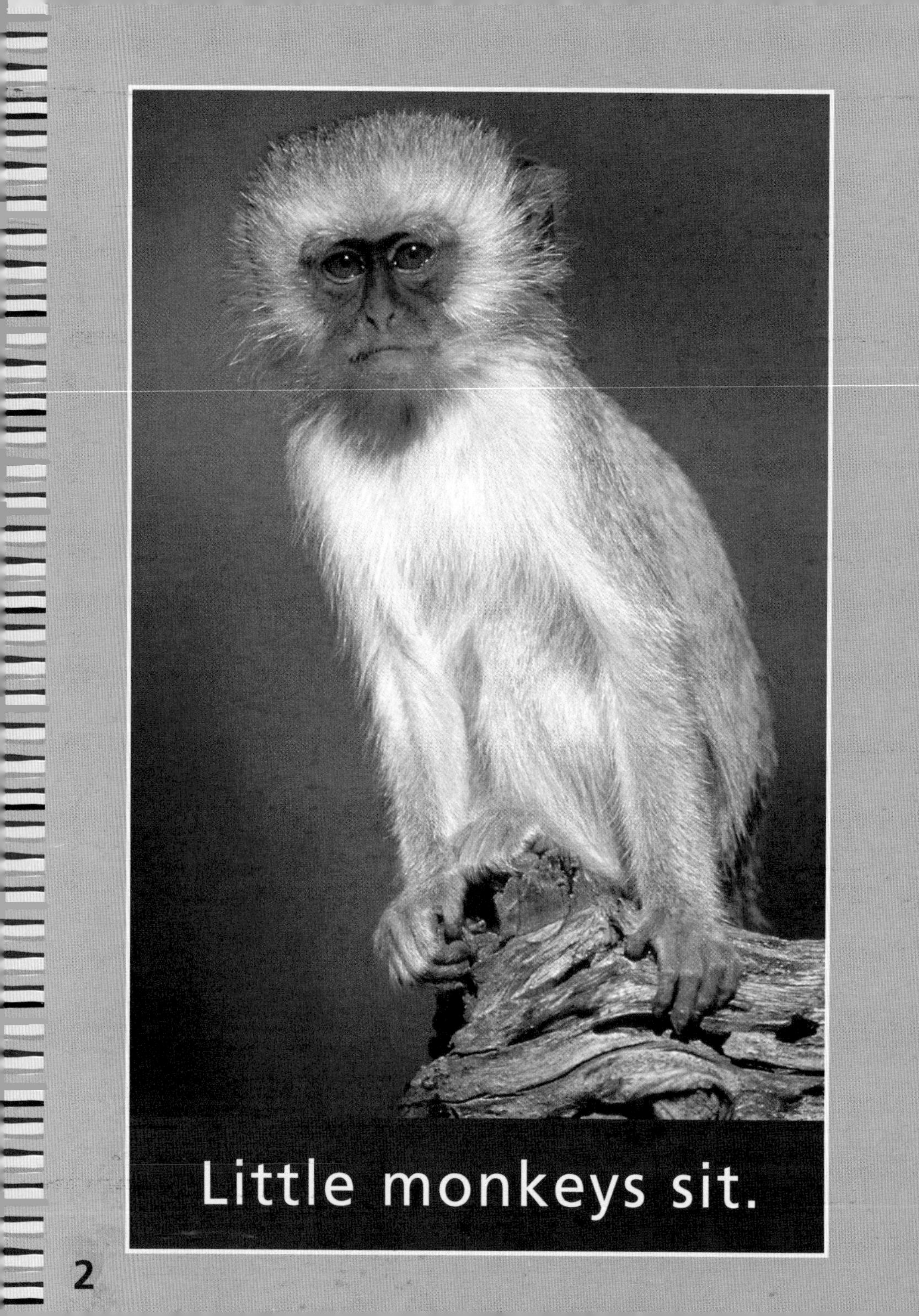

Little monkeys sit.

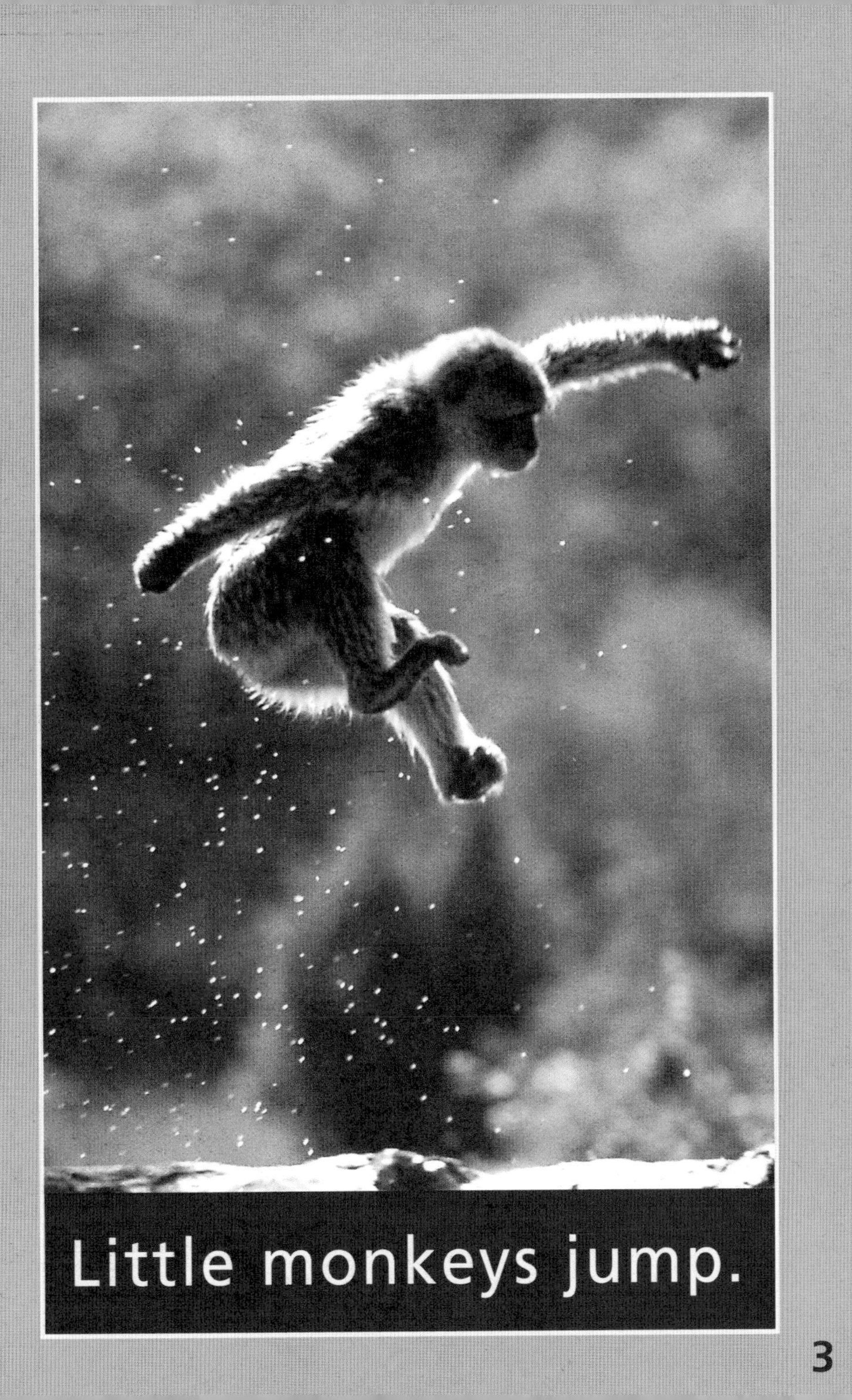

Little monkeys jump.

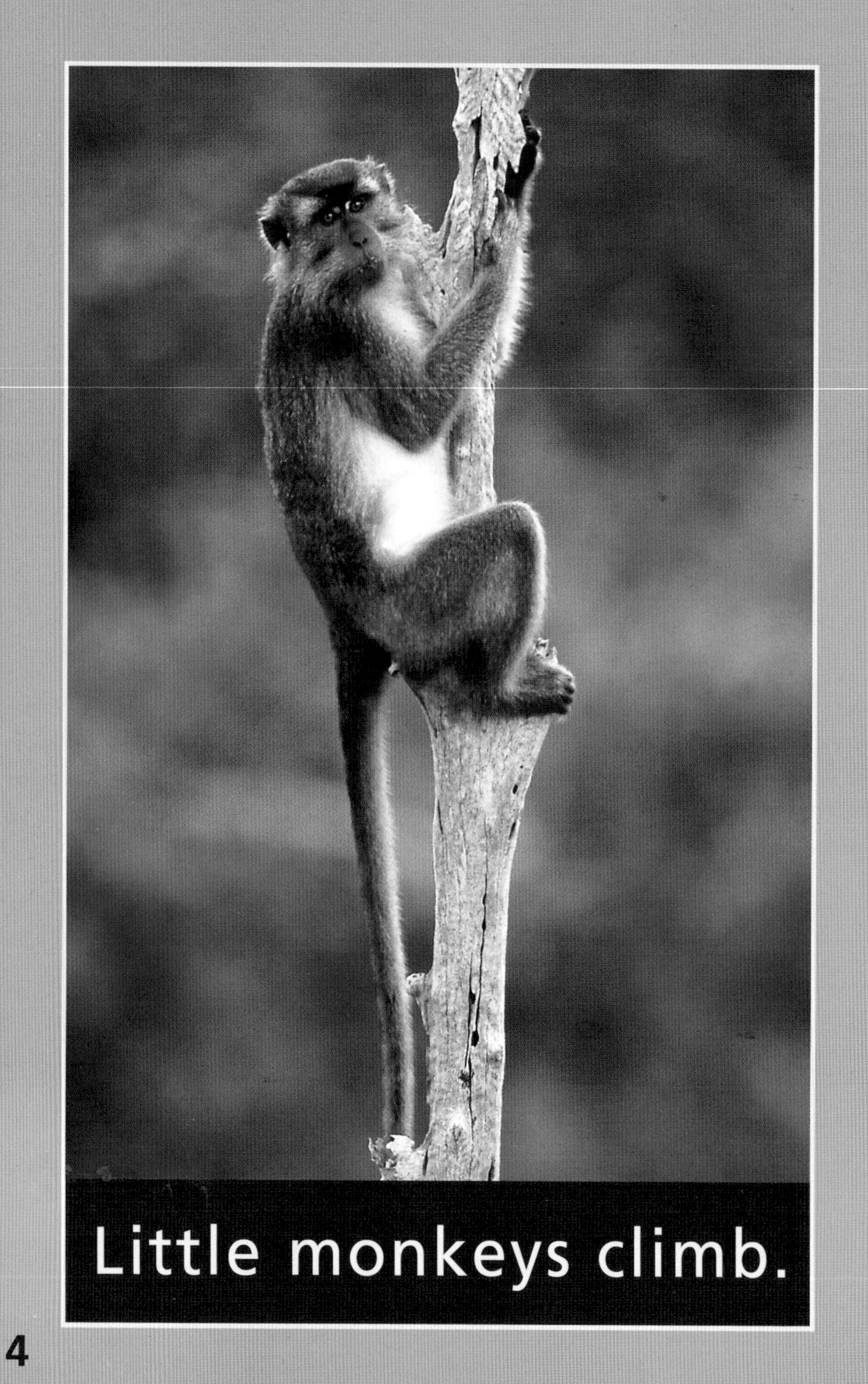

Little monkeys climb.

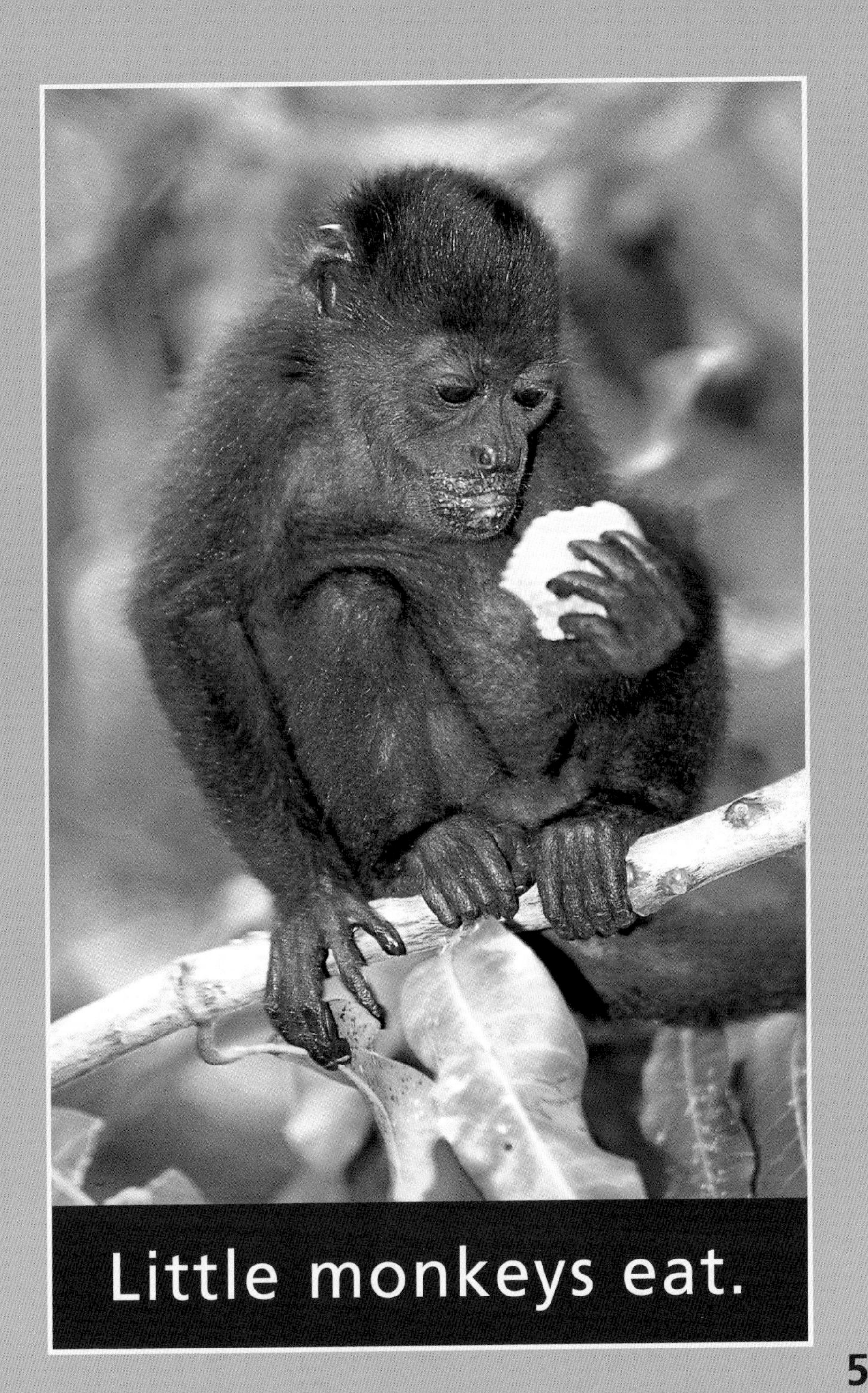

Little monkeys eat.

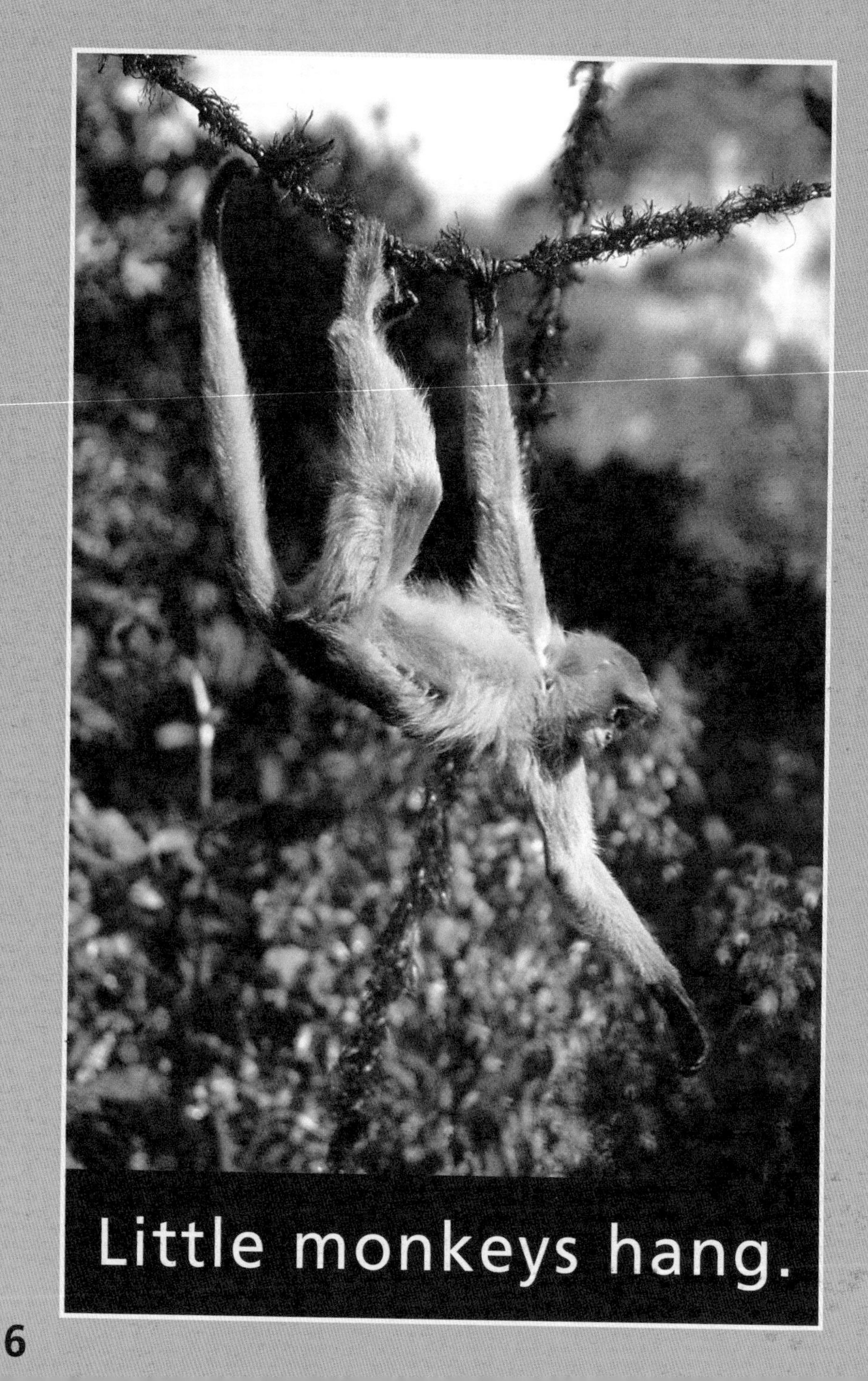

Little monkeys hang.

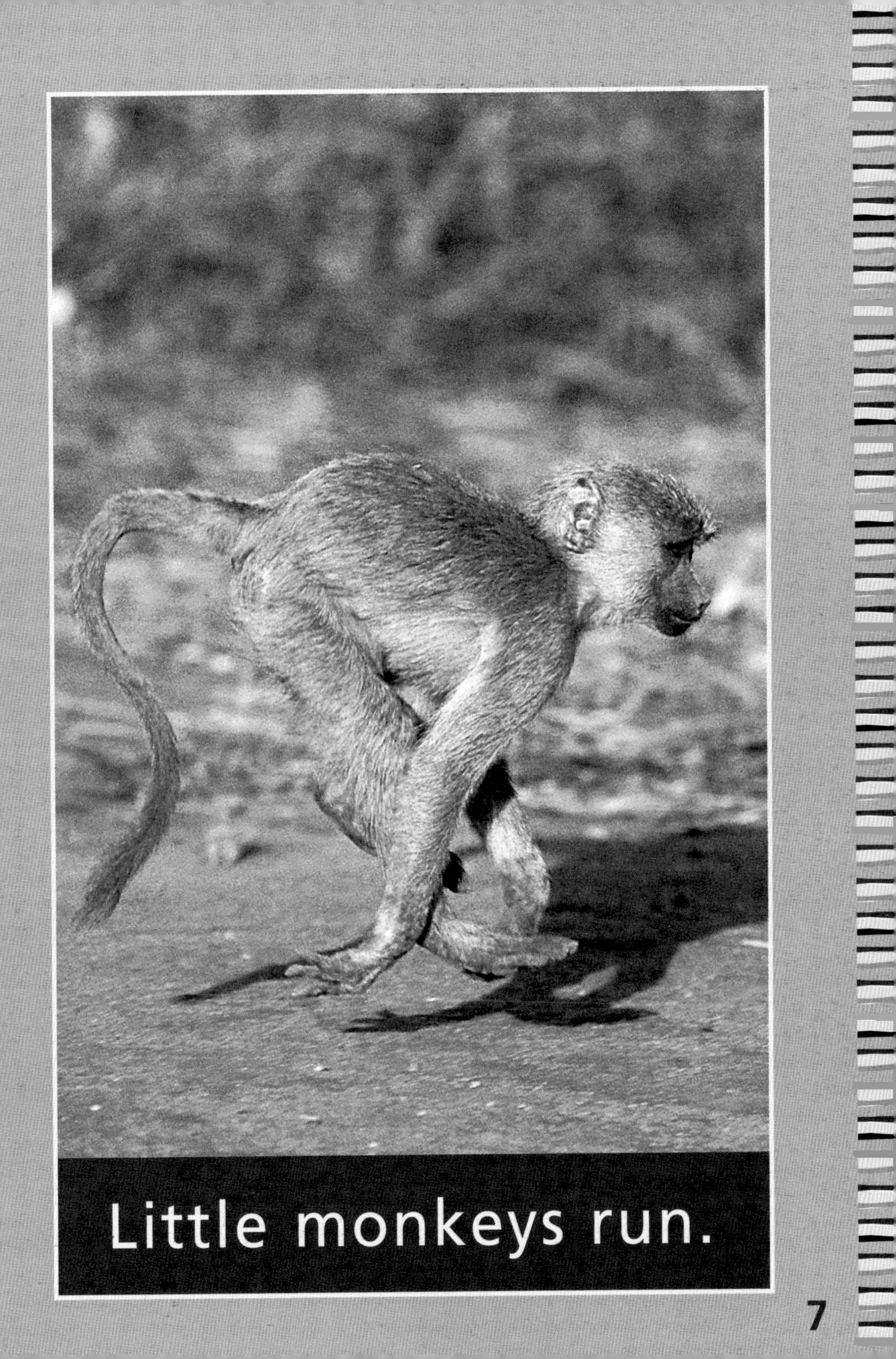

Little monkeys run.

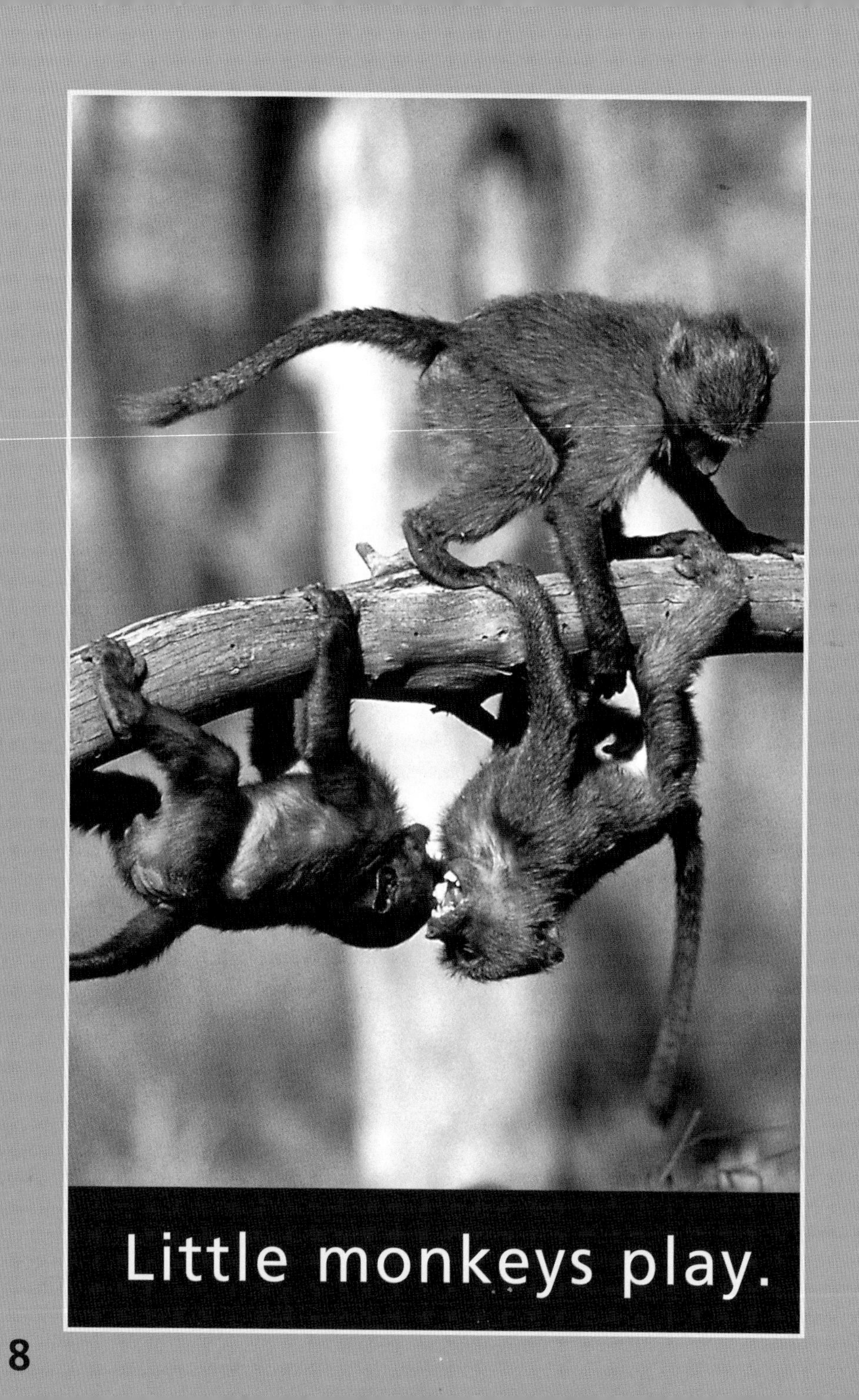

Little monkeys play.